3

Fact Cat

POLES

Izzi Howell

WAYLAND

FACT CAT

Get your paws on this fantastic new mega-series from Wayland!

Join our Fact Cat on a journey of fun learning about every subject under the sun!

First published in Great Britain in 2015 by Wayland
ISBN: 978 0 7502 9022 7
Library ebook ISBN: 978 0 7502 9023 4
Dewey Number: 910.9'11-dc23

10 9 8 7 6 5 4 3 2 1

Wayland
An imprint of Hachette Children's Group
Part of Hodder & Stoughton
Carmelite House
50 Victoria Embankment
London EC4Y 0DZ

An Hachette UK Company
www.hachette.co.uk
www.hachettechildrens.co.uk

A catalogue for this title is available from
the British Library
Printed and bound in China

Produced for Wayland by
White-Thomson Publishing Ltd
www.wtpub.co.uk

Editor: Izzi Howell
Design: Rocket Design (East Anglia) Ltd
Fact Cat illustrations: Shutterstock/Julien Troneur
Other illustrations: Stefan Chabluk
Consultant: Kate Ruttle

Picture and illustration credits:
Corbis: Galen Rowell (cover), Hulton-Deutsch Collection 14; iStock: Mlenny (title page), Imgorthand 10, JohnPitcher 12, KeithSzafranski 13; Science Photo Library: Scott Polar Reseach Institute 15; Shutterstock: Kundra 4 (left) and 5 (right), BMJ 6, Dudarev Mikhail 9, Tilo G 11, Grigorii Pisotsckii 16, Josef Pittner 17, DonLand 20; Stefan Chabluk: 4 (right) and 5 (centre); Thinkstock: goinyk 7, SlobodanMiljevic 21; U.S. Antarctic Program: Deven Stross/National Science Foundation 5 (right), Kristina 'Kricket' Scheerer/ National Science Foundation 8, Timothy Russer/TSGT/USAF/National Science Foundation 18 (top), Peter Rejcek/National Science Foundation 18 (bottom), Peter Rejcek/National Science Foundation 19.

Every effort has been made to clear copyright. Should there be any inadvertent omission, please apply to the publisher for rectification.

The author, Izzi Howell, is a writer and editor specialising in children's educational publishing.

The consultant, Kate Ruttle, is a literacy expert and SENCO, and teaches in Suffolk.

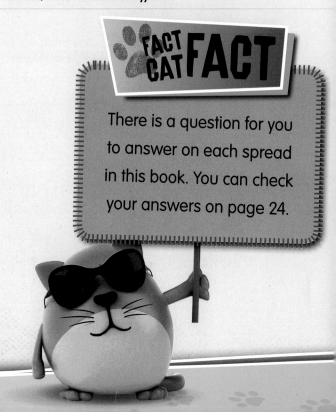

FACT CAT FACT

There is a question for you to answer on each spread in this book. You can check your answers on page 24.

CONTENTS

WHERE ARE THE POLES?

The North Pole is the point on Earth that is furthest north. It is found in the middle of the Arctic Ocean, to the north of Canada, Greenland and Russia.

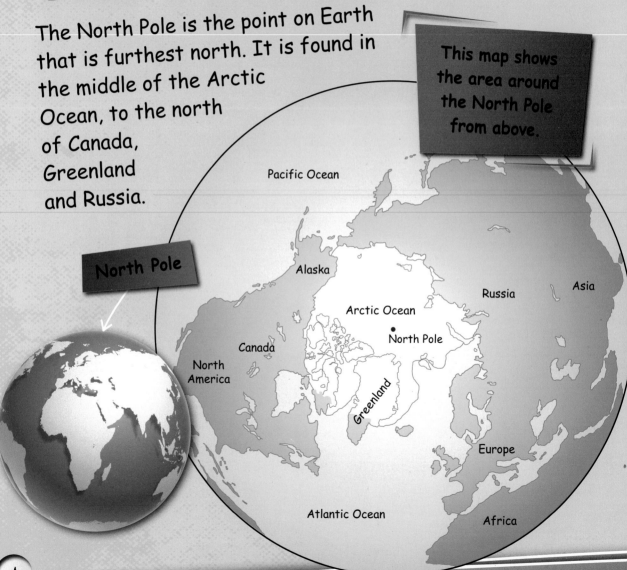

This map shows the area around the North Pole from above.

North Pole

Pacific Ocean

Alaska

Arctic Ocean

Russia

Asia

North Pole

Canada

North America

Greenland

Europe

Atlantic Ocean

Africa

The southernmost point on Earth is called the South Pole. The South Pole is near the centre of Antarctica, one of Earth's seven **continents**.

South America is the closest continent to Antarctica. Find out which two countries make up the southern tip of South America.

Atlantic Ocean

South America

Southern Ocean

Antarctica

South Pole•

Southern Ocean

Pacific Ocean

Australia

New Zealand

South Pole

FACT CAT FACT

This post marks the exact point of the South Pole in Antarctica. There is no marker for the North Pole, because it is in the middle of the ocean!

LAND

There is no land under the ice at the North Pole. The Arctic Ocean is covered by a thick **ice cap** that humans and animals can walk on. The area on top of the ice cap is called the Arctic.

This bearded seal is resting on the ice in the Arctic Ocean.

At the South Pole, there is land under the ice and snow. A mountain range goes through the centre of Antarctica, passing close to the South Pole.

The Transantarctic Mountains make up one of the longest **mountain ranges** on Earth. Find out how long it is.

FACT CAT FACT

Millions of years ago, dinosaurs lived in Antarctica. Dinosaur **fossils** have been found on Mount Kirkpatrick in the Transantarctic Mountains.

WEATHER

Antarctica is the coldest area on Earth. Near the South Pole, the temperature is normally around -50 °C, but it can get as cold as -82 °C. By the coast, the weather is warmer.

It's so cold in Antarctica that your tears can **freeze** and stick your eyelashes together!

The Arctic is much warmer than Antarctica because of the Arctic Ocean. The water under the ice makes the **surface** temperature higher. The coldest temperature ever recorded on the surface of the Arctic ice was -40 °C.

Some people are brave enough to swim in the chilly Arctic Ocean! Find out the temperature that water freezes at.

FACT CAT FACT

It's so cold at the poles that if you throw a cup of hot water into the air, it falls to the ground as snow!

SEASONS

During the summer in the polar regions, it doesn't get dark at night. It stays light all day and all night for several months.

Children that live in the polar regions can play outside until late at night during the summer, as the sun never sets.

The sun doesn't rise during the winter months at the poles. There is no sunlight. It is dark all day and all night.

These houses in the far north of Norway have their electric lights switched on all winter, as there is no natural light.

FACT CAT FACT

When it is summer at the North Pole, it is winter at the South Pole. This is because the poles are in different **hemispheres**. Find out which hemisphere the North Pole is in.

WILDLIFE

At the North Pole, large **mammals**, such as polar bears, live on the ice. Polar bears are strong swimmers. They can swim for hours in the cold Arctic Ocean.

Many Arctic animals have white **fur** for **camouflage**.

FACT CAT FACT

Even though polar bears have bright white fur, their skin is black. It helps to keep them warm, because dark colours take in more heat from the sun.

Penguins are one of the few animals that live in Antarctica. The weather is too cold for most land animals. However, fish and other ocean animals live in the Southern Ocean, which **surrounds** Antarctica.

Emperor penguins come on to land to lay eggs and take care of their young. Find out another type of penguin that lives in Antarctica.

EXPLORING THE POLES

The American explorer Robert Peary was probably the first person to reach the North Pole, in 1909. He travelled with a team of 23 men, including several **Inuit guides**.

The Inuit taught Peary how to **survive** in the Arctic. He learned to wear warm animal furs to keep out the cold.

In December 1911, the Norwegian explorer Roald Amundsen and his team were the first people to reach the South Pole. Their journey by dog sled from their base camp in Antarctica took more than two months.

Amundsen left a Norwegian flag at the pole to show that he had arrived first. The British explorer Robert Falcon Scott reached the South Pole in January 1912, one month after Amundsen.

FACT CAT FACT

Roald Amundsen also travelled to the North Pole, making him the first person to visit both poles. Find out in which year Amundsen visited the North Pole.

PEOPLE IN THE ARCTIC

No-one lives at the North Pole, but people do live in the Arctic Circle. The Arctic Circle is an area that includes the north of countries such as Canada, Russia and Greenland.

The Nenets **tribe** live in Siberia, in the far north of Russia. These Nenets women are wearing traditional coats called Yagushkas, made from eight layers of reindeer skin.

Very few plants grow in the Arctic Circle, so Arctic tribes mainly eat meat and fish. In the past, people living in the Arctic had to catch their own food. Today, some towns have shops selling groceries.

In the north of Canada, the Inuit still eat caribou and seals. Find out what the Inuit word for seal is.

FACT CAT FACT

The Nenets cut holes in the Arctic ice to catch fish from the ocean below. The unfrozen ocean is actually warmer than the air, so some Nenets put their hands in the water to warm them up!

PEOPLE IN ANTARCTICA

Scientists come to Antarctica every summer to do experiments. They live in **huts** on research bases.

McMurdo Station is the largest research base in Antarctica, with a **population** of over 1,000 people in the summer. Find out the name of another polar research base.

When scientists need to do experiments far from their research base, they live and work in tents.

Antarctica is a good place to do experiments because it doesn't have much **pollution**. Some scientists in Antarctica study the air that we breathe. Others use telescopes to look at the stars.

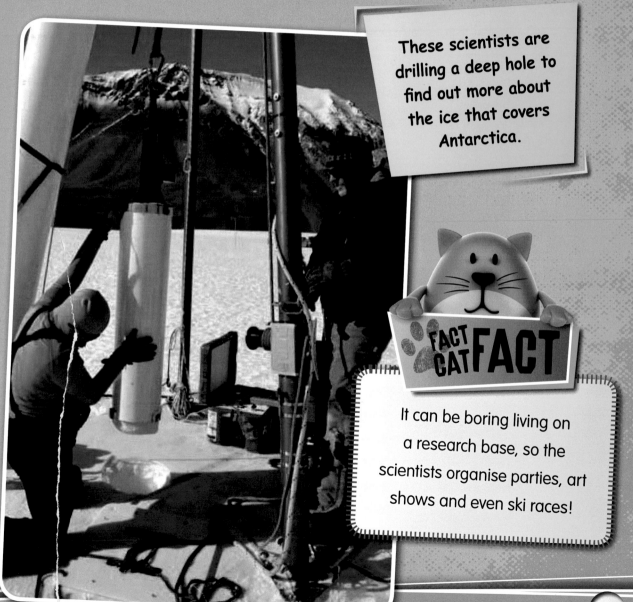

These scientists are drilling a deep hole to find out more about the ice that covers Antarctica.

FACT CAT FACT

It can be boring living on a research base, so the scientists organise parties, art shows and even ski races!

THE FUTURE

The ice caps at the North and South Poles are **melting** because the temperature on Earth is getting hotter. Scientists worry that if the Earth keeps getting warmer, all the ice at the poles will melt away.

Polar bears hunt on the ice. If the ice melts, it will be harder for polar bears to find food. Find out what polar bears eat.

When ice melts, it turns to water. The extra water from the melting ice caps will make **sea levels** rise around the world.

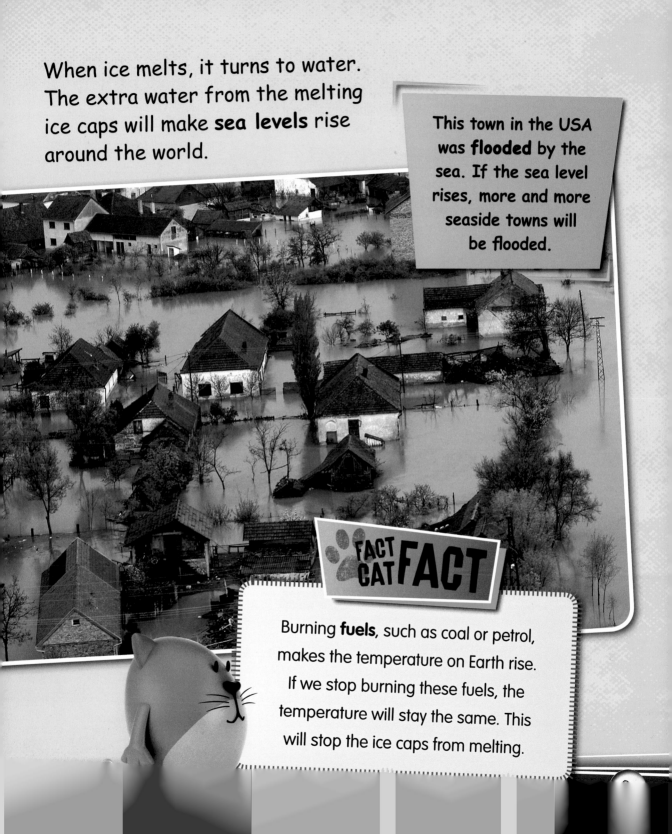

This town in the USA was **flooded** by the sea. If the sea level rises, more and more seaside towns will be flooded.

FACT CAT FACT

Burning **fuels**, such as coal or petrol, makes the temperature on Earth rise. If we stop burning these fuels, the temperature will stay the same. This will stop the ice caps from melting.

QUIZ Try to answer the questions below. Look back through the book to help you. Check your answers on page 24.

1 Which continent is the South Pole in?

a) Africa

b) South America

c) Antarctica

2 There is land under the North Pole. True or not true?

a) true

b) not true

3 What colour is polar bears' skin?

a) Black

b) White

c) Grey

4 Roald Amundsen and his team were the first people to reach the South Pole. True or not true?

a) true

b) not true

5 Where does the Nenets tribe live?

a) Greenland

b) Siberia

c) Antarctica

6 There are research bases in Antarctica. True or not true?

a) true

b) not true

GLOSSARY

camouflage hiding by making yourself the same colour as the area that you are in

continent one of the seven main areas of land on Earth, such as Africa or North America

experiment a test that you do to learn or find out something

flood when water covers an area that is usually dry

fossil part of an animal or a plant from thousands of years ago preserved in rock

freeze when water turns to ice

fuel something we burn to make power or heat

fur the hair of an animal

guide someone whose job is to show people how to get somewhere

hemisphere one half of the Earth

hut a small building

ice cap a layer of ice covering an area

Inuit a tribe of people who live in the north of Canada, Greenland and Alaska

mammal an animal, such as a cow or a monkey, that feeds its young with milk from its body

melt to turn from a solid to a liquid because of heat

mountain range a group of mountains

pollution damage caused to nature by rubbish or dangerous chemicals

population the number of people living in an area

research base a building where scientists live and do experiments

sea level the distance between the sea floor and the surface of the sea

surface the top part of something

surround to be around something

survive to stay alive

tribe a group of people who live together

INDEX

ANSWERS

Pages 5-20

Page 5: Argentina and Chile

Page 7: 3,500 km

Page 9: 0°C

Page 11: the Northern Hemisphere

Page 13: Adélie penguins

Page 15: 1926

Page 17: Nattiq

Page 18: Some bases include the Amundsen-Scott South Pole Station and the Halley Research Station

Page 20: Mostly ringed and bearded seals

Quiz answers

1 c) Antarctica

2 b) not true – it is on an ice cap in the Arctic Ocean

3 a) black

4 a) true

5 b) Siberia

6 a) true

OTHER TITLES IN THE FACT CAT SERIES...

Space
The Earth 978 0 7502 8220 8
The Moon 978 0 7502 8221 5
The Planets 978 0 7502 8222 2
The Sun 978 0 7502 8223 9

United Kingdom
England 978 0 7502 8433 2
Northern Ireland 978 0 7502 8440 0
Scotland 978 0 7502 8439 4
Wales 978 0 7502 8438 7

Countries
Brazil 978 0 7502 8213 0
France 978 0 7502 8212 3
Ghana 978 0 7502 8215 4
Italy 978 0 7502 8214 7

History
Neil Armstrong 978 0 7502 9040 1
Amelia Earhart 978 0 7502 9034 0
Christopher Columbus 978 0 7502 9031 9
The Wright Brothers 978 0 7502 9037 1

Habitats
Ocean 978 0 7502 8218 5
Rainforest 978 0 7502 8219 2
Seashore 978 0 7502 8216 1
Woodland 978 0 7502 8217 8

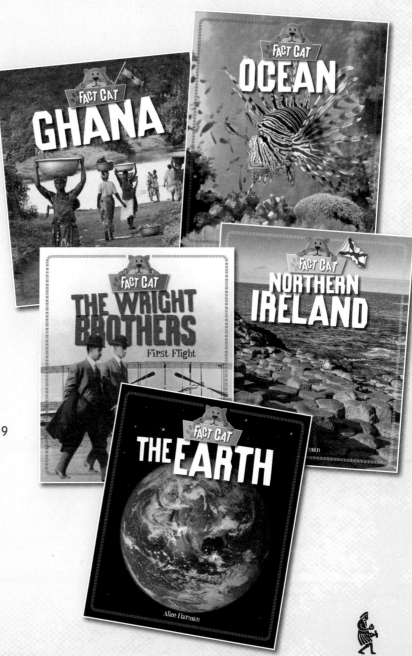

WAYLAND